WORLD FEATURE FOCUS

SETTLEMENTS

Rebecca Kahn

W
FRANKLIN WATTS
LONDON • SYDNEY

CONTENTS

page 8

page 22

page 12

page 20

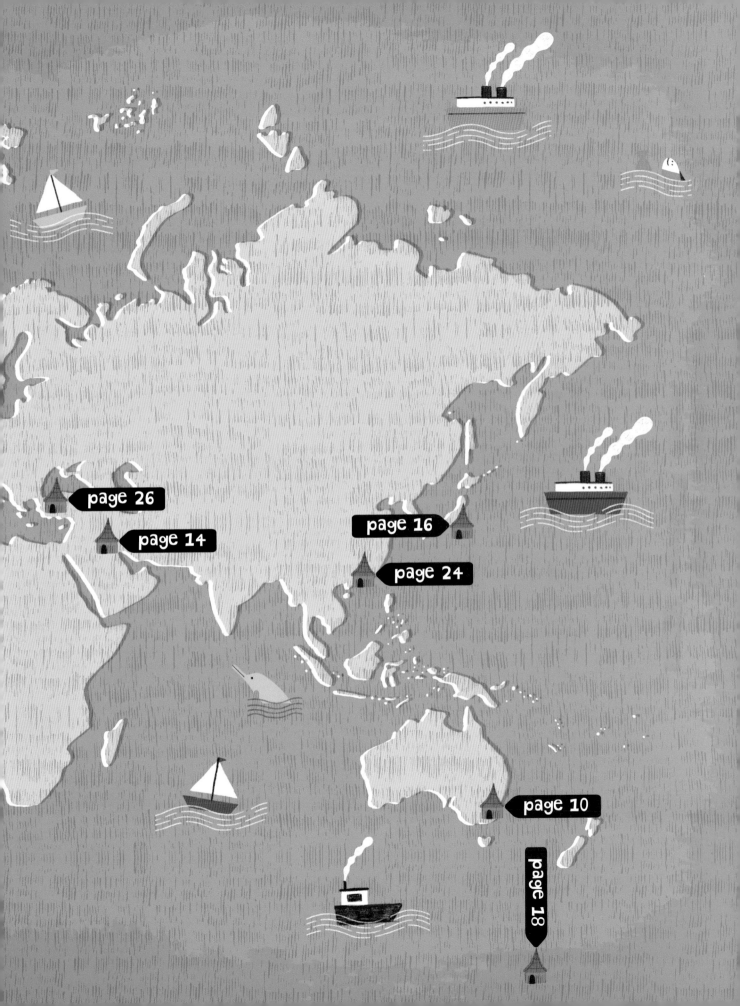

SETTLEMENTS AROUND THE WORLD

Human beings have always lived together in groups. In the past, this made it easier to defend themselves against predators and enemies, and to share food and other resources. Over time, as people learnt how to farm and built permanent homes, some of these settlements grew into hamlets, villages, towns, cities and even megalopolises.

Here is an introduction to the main types of settlement and some geographical words that you will come across in the rest of the book.

HAMLET

A hamlet is a small settlement. It is made up of a few houses, often with no shops or other services. A hamlet usually provides homes for farmers or fishermen, or sometimes serves a place of employment, such as a mill or a quarry.

The edge of a small hamlet in the Chiltern Hills in the UK.

VILLAGE

A village is a settlement which is larger than a hamlet but smaller than a town. Many villages are surrounded by countryside. The streets are often arranged around a marketplace or public square. Some villages developed along a road or river.

A small village by Lake Dal in the north of India.

TOWN

Towns are settlements which are larger than villages, but smaller than cities. A town can usually support its own economy, meaning some of the people who live there also work in the town. A town has shops, parks and schools, and may have a hospital, police station or railway station.

The Dutch town of Elburg began as a small Neolithic settlement which grew to become a wealthy medieval town.

CITY

A city is a large settlement. Its situation, such as being close to an important port, has led to it becoming home to many people. Cities have shops, businesses, factories, government offices, public transport systems, housing and places to have fun. Over half of the world's population live in cities.

The business district of Jakarta, the capital of Indonesia.

MEGALOPOLIS

A megalopolis is an area where some cities or large towns have grown towards each other to form an uninterrupted urban area. These super cities are home to many millions of people, who travel around by road, rail and underground train.

New York City is part of the USA's northeast megalopolis, which stretches up the coast to Boston and down to Washington DC. It is home to over 50 million people.

RURAL

Rural is the word used to describe an area with a small population living in scattered settlements. A rural landscape could be grassland, forest, savannah or desert. Most people live in isolated houses, hamlets or villages in rural areas.

The rural parts of Guangxi region in China have small settlements as well as rivers and mountains.

URBAN

Urban areas are towns and cities with large populations, where people live close together in streets, housing estates and high-rise flats. They need a lot of infrastructure, such as buildings, transport systems, power supplies, tunnels and bridges, as well as schools, hospitals, parks, sports facilities and places of employment.

China's capital city, Beijing, is one of the worlds's most populated cities, and it continues to grow.

URBANISATION

These new houses have been built to house a growing population. Solar panels on their roofs will provide them with renewable energy.

This term describes the process where a rural settlement grows into an urban settlement, or an urban settlement grows bigger.

CONURBATION

A conurbation is a city that has expanded into surrounding smaller cities, towns and villages to become one big settlement under a single name. For instance, within the San Francisco Bay Area conurbation in the USA are the cities of San Francisco, Berkeley and Oakland.

The San Francisco Bay Area has a population of about 8 million, while the actual city of San Francisco has a population of about 800,000.

INFRASTRUCTURE

Infrastructure is the services and facilities that support a settlement, such as clean water, electricity, broadband and waste disposal, as well as schools, hospitals, roads, bridges, railways and airports.

These cooling towers are part of a power plant that supplies energy to settlements in the Czech Republic.

SKARA BRAE

Skara Brae is a 5,000-year-old Neolithic settlement on Orkney, off the north coast of Scotland. The village was discovered in 1850, when a huge storm uncovered the remains of nine houses.

UNUSUAL WALLS

The houses were built into mounds of waste, known as middens. These consisted mostly of animal bones, plant matter and seashells. The walls provided stability, some insulation and shelter from the weather. They helped to protect the village for thousands of years.

HOUSES

The houses were built of slabs of stone with a roof held up by a wooden post or whalebone. Each house had a large main room, with a fire burning in the centre.

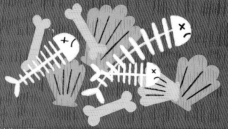

COMMUNITY

Each house in Skara Brae had a door, allowing the people inside to close it and have some privacy. All the houses were connected by covered passageways. No weapons have been found, suggesting that Skara Brae was a peaceful place to live.

STONE FURNITURE

All the houses were fitted with similar stone furniture: a stone table, a dresser, a cupboard, two stone box beds, a hearth and storage tanks. There were few trees on Orkney so inhabitants had to use stone.

FARMLAND

When it was built, Skara Brae was beside an inland loch, but coastal erosion has brought the sea right to the edge of the settlement. From the contents of their rubbish, we know that the people who lived there were farmers, who kept animals and grew barley.

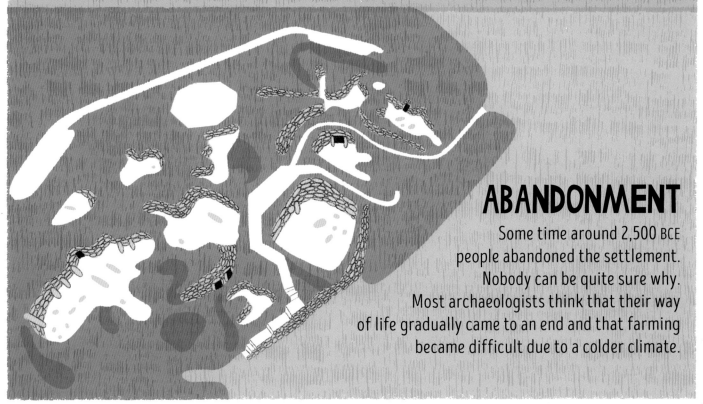

ABANDONMENT

Some time around 2,500 BCE people abandoned the settlement. Nobody can be quite sure why. Most archaeologists think that their way of life gradually came to an end and that farming became difficult due to a colder climate.

JUNEE

During the 19th century, railway companies started to build railway tracks across Australia. Towns such as Junee, in New South Wales, Australia, sprung up around railway junctions. It is on the railway route linking Sydney to Melbourne.

SMALL TOWN

Today, Junee is a town with a population of about 6,000 people. Before European settlers arrived, the Wiradjuri Aborigines lived in the area. By the 1840s, a few sheep farmers had settled there. The hamlet became an important stop on the wool route to Sydney, used to transport goods.

Sydney
Junee•
Melbourne•

GOLD RUSH

By the mid 1860s, gold had been discovered near Junee. The hamlet of Junee grew into a village as prospectors arrived to try their luck in the mines. By the late 1870s, there was a school, a hotel, a post office and a church in the settlement.

RAILWAY BOOM

In 1878, the Great Southern Railway reached the area, passing east of the village. The railway link to Sydney meant that farmers could transport their goods much more easily. The village grew into a boom town.

GROWING

As the population increased, so did the town. Schools, post offices, a bank, a court house and businesses opened during the 1880s and 1890s, providing services.

STILL A TOWN

Junee thrived, becoming an important railway depot in the mid 20th century. Even when the depot closed, Junee survived by encouraging tourism and supporting local industries.

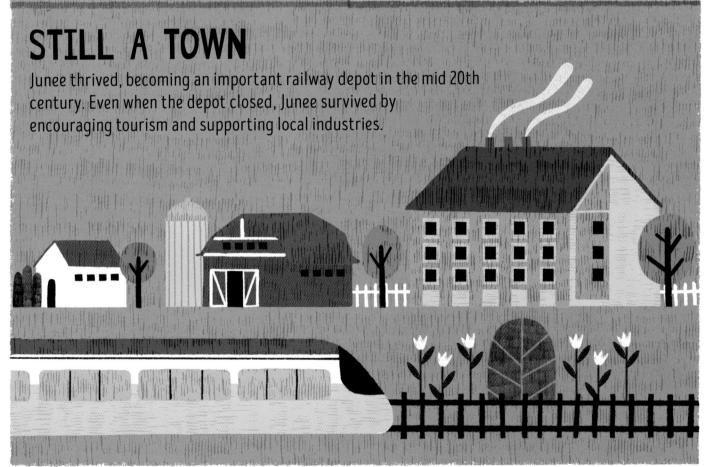

SAN DIEGO-TIJUANA

The cities of San Diego in California, USA, and Tijuana in Mexico form an international conurbation either side of the Mexico-USA border. Together they cover 16,000 square kilometres.

INTERNATIONAL CONURBATION

The San Diego-Tijuana international conurbation is home to almost five million people and is still growing. It has many businesses providing jobs, as well as the port of San Diego, home to the Pacific Fleet of the US Navy.

CROSSING BORDERS

Every year over fifty million people use the San Ysidro border to cross between the USA and Mexico at San Diego-Tijuana. It is the busiest land border crossing in the world.

SHARED INFRASTRUCTURE

San Diego-Tijuana share many things, including their sewage! The International Boundary Wastewater Treatment Plant purifies waste water from both cities.

CHANGING COUNTRIES

Many businesses have their factories in Tijuana and their offices in San Diego to benefit from lower wages in Mexico. So people might work in a different country to the one they live in, and many children cross the border to go to school every day.

FRUITFUL LAND

The area has a warm climate, ideal for growing crops, although the cost of water can be high as there is low rainfall. Avocados, strawberries and grapes for wine are all grown in the area.

GETTING IN AND OUT

San Diego-Tijuana is connected to the rest of the USA and Mexico by many busy motorways, three international airports and a large port. These convenient routes in and out of both sides of the conurbation have helped it to grow.

CTESIPHON

Sometimes settlements are abandoned. There can be different reasons for this, such as war or extreme weather. The ancient city of Ctesiphon in Iraq, flourished for about eight hundred years before it fell into ruins.

ANCIENT CITY

Ctesiphon was the capital city of the Parthian and then the Sasanian empires between 51 BCE and CE 637. All that is left of this great city are the ruins of the royal palace of Taq Kasra, which has the largest unsupported arch in the world.

GOOD SPOT

Ctesiphon's site on the banks of the River Tigris and on the Royal Road, an ancient highway, was ideal. Being on the river and trade route gave the rulers of Ctesiphon control over trade and travel as well as access to water in a very dry region.

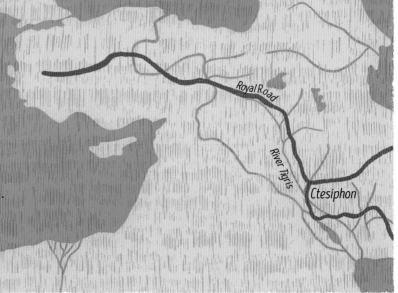

Royal Road

River Tigris

Ctesiphon

MYSTERIOUS HISTORY

A 7th century bowl, showing a Sasanian king going hunting.

Although Ctesiphon was attacked by the Roman army five times over its six-hundred-year history, the Parthian and Sasanian rulers kept their power. Very little has survived from Ctesiphon itself but there are sculptures, metalwork, mosaics, jewellery and ceramics from other parts of the Parthian Empire.

ANCIENT DIVERSITY

A rich city populated by Muslims, Christians and Jews, Ctesiphon flourished until 637 when it was finally conquered by invaders, who moved the capital to Baghdad. The city was soon abandoned, and bricks and stones were taken from the great buildings to be used to build other cities.

MORE BATTLES

Since it fell into ruins, the site of Ctesiphon has seen many battles, including the Battle of Ctesiphon in 1915 during the First World War (1914-1918).

AOGASHIMA

Some people have made their homes in dangerous places. The inhabitants of the small Japanese island of Aogashima live inside the crater of an active volcano in the Philippine Sea.

VOLCANO HOME

How and why a settlement formed inside the volcano is unknown. It is one of the most isolated human settlements in the world, home to just over 160 people living in a village that has been around for at least five hundred years.

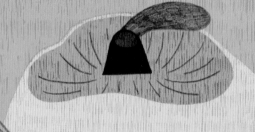

Tokyo

Izu Ōshima

Miyake

Mikurajima

ARCHIPELAGO

Aogashima is part of the Izu Islands, an archipelago off the south-west coast of Japan.

Nine of the islands in the group are inhabited, and Aogashima is the most remote.

Hachijyo

Aogashima

FISHING

Surrounded by the Philippine Sea, fishing is one of the main livelihoods of the people of Aogashima. Other occupations are farming, salt production and a few office jobs.

HOT SPRINGS

Geothermal energy from the volcano creates lots of hot springs on this island. Locals have created several naturally heated saunas. In some places people can use the steam vents from the volcano to boil eggs and other snacks.

IT'S ALIVE!

Although the Japanese government classifies the volcano as active, it has been 230 years since it erupted. Many residents are happy to take this risk in order to live in such a calm, beautiful place.

GETTING AROUND

To reach Tokyo, the capital of Japan, villagers can take a 350-km journey by ferry. However the port cannot be used during bad weather, so people often travel by helicopter. On the island, it can be wet and windy so people get around by car.

McMURDO STATION

Research stations are often in remote locations and can be found in some of the most extreme climates. The continent of Antarctica is uninhabited apart for the scientists and support workers who live at McMurdo Station.

FIRST VISITORS

McMurdo is named after Lieutenant Archibald McMurdo, a British Royal Navy commander who took part in an expedition to map the Antarctic in 1841. Sixty years later, the Discovery Expedition of 1901-1904, led by Captain Robert Scott, returned to the area. They built a small wooden hut, called Discovery Hut, to store food and supplies and it still stands today.

RESEARCH

McMurdo Station is home to the United States Antarctic Research Programme. It has a population of about 1,200 during the summer, falling to about 250 people over the winter. It has a harbour, three airfields, a heliport, laboratories, living spaces, a coffee shop and a bar.

FROZEN FOOD

Every year, the US military co-ordinates Operation Deep Freeze - a delivery of 42 million litres of fuel and five million kg of supplies sent to the community by ship. The supplies include food, as well as medical and scientific equipment.

DAILY WORK

Scientists at McMurdo Station study astrophysics, biology, medicine, oceans, geology and climate change. They usually spend a few months there over the summer. The support staff (plumbers, IT experts, cooks) often live there all year.

KEEPING BUSY

It could easily get boring in McMurdo, where winter temperatures can drop to -30°C. However, as well as working on their research or support jobs, McMurdo residents use the gyms, take part in regular sporting events, such as rugby or basketball matches, go to lectures, learn new skills and meet friends in the coffee shop or bar.

UROS ISLANDS

Many settlements develop near water, but there are some places where people actually build their homes on water. Lake Titicaca in South America is one such place, home to the Uros people of Peru who live on floating islands.

FLOATING ISLANDS

The Uros have lived on the lake for hundreds of years. Each island starts as a block of earth, onto which woven mats of tortora reeds are added in layers. Each island has between three and ten houses on it, forming a small village.

HOME BUILDING

Every few months, new dried reeds are added on top of the islands to keep them dry and strong. Each island lasts for about thirty years.

VITAL CROP

Reeds are the most important crop for the Uros people. As well as providing materials to build their islands and homes, they weave the reeds into boats, used for fishing and hunting, and into handicrafts to sell to tourists.

cormorant

ibis

domestic cat

FLOATING FARMS

The Uros keep cattle and graze them on the islands. They have trained cormorants to catch fish for them and they keep ibis for laying eggs. Many families keep cats to catch rats that might damage their reed island homes.

SAFETY

The floating islands were originally built as a way for the Uros to defend themselves. If they were in danger, the islands could be cut loose and float away. At least one island has a watchtower made entirely of reeds, to watch out for danger.

LAS VEGAS

Many human settlements have developed along trade routes, important roads or rivers linking towns and cities. Las Vegas in Nevada, USA grew from tiny beginnings into a vast modern city.

SMALL BEGINNINGS

Las Vegas gets its name from the Spanish word for 'meadows', due to the wild grasses and freshwater springs once found there. The water supply and grass made it a convenient place for people to stop for a break when they were travelling in covered horse-drawn wagons between New Mexico and California.

PACK STOP

A town grew up, providing a useful stopping place for pack-trains, groups of horses, mules and donkeys that carried goods and letters. Since there were no railways or roads along the trail at this time, pack animals were the only way to cross the harsh, semi-desert landscape.

LIGHT IN THE DESERT

Nowadays, Las Vegas is mostly known for its tourist attractions, bright lights, flashy buildings and fountains ...

... but close by, Red Rock Canyon is a reminder that this city is built in the Mojave Desert.

SAVING WATER

The many fountains and man-made lakes in Las Vegas use grey water, which is recycled water from people's showers, baths and sinks. This helps to conserve water in the arid landscape.

LIGHTS AND WATER

Las Vegas gets most of its water supply from Lake Mead, the largest reservoir in the USA. It was formed when part of the Colorado river was dammed to build the Hoover Dam. The dam has a large hydroelectric power station, providing Las Vegas with electricity.

HONG KONG

Some communities build their settlements high into the air. This is usually due to lack of space. The city of Hong Kong occupies Hong Kong Island, some smaller islands and a bit of the Chinese mainland.

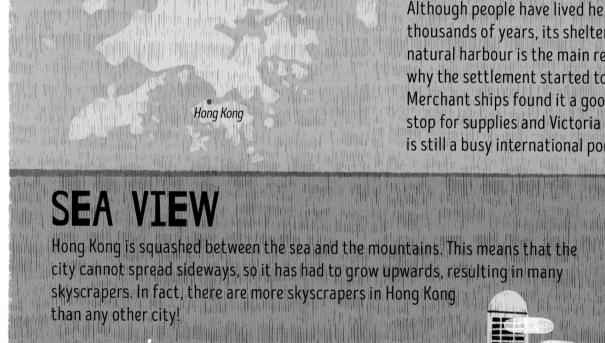

Hong Kong

HARBOUR CITY

Although people have lived here for thousands of years, its sheltered natural harbour is the main reason why the settlement started to grow. Merchant ships found it a good place to stop for supplies and Victoria Harbour is still a busy international port.

SEA VIEW

Hong Kong is squashed between the sea and the mountains. This means that the city cannot spread sideways, so it has had to grow upwards, resulting in many skyscrapers. In fact, there are more skyscrapers in Hong Kong than any other city!

GROWING UP

In Hong Kong, more people live and work above the 14th floor of their building than anywhere else in the world. This makes it the world's most vertical city. Homes are very expensive, so most families live in small flats.

SKY FARMING

Because there is so little space around the city, and the hillsides are too steep for farming, Hong Kong has to import most of its food from mainland China. Only about 7 km of land in Hong Kong is used for farming. Increasingly, people use their roofs and balconies to grow fruit and vegetables.

TINY HOMES

Hong Kong is one of the most densely populated cities in the world. About six thousand people live in every square kilometre. Some of the poorest people live in one-room 'coffin homes', often only as long and as wide as a single bed.

KAYMAKLI

Sometimes people decide to live under the ground as protection from weather or enemies. These settlements require special building skills to keep people healthy and safe. Kaymakli in Turkey is an ancient underground city built as a place of safety to hide from attackers.

SAFELY UNDERGROUND

Archaeologists think that the Phrygians, who lived in the area over 2,700 years ago, started to build Kaymakli out of the soft rock of Cappadocia. Others continued the work, building hundreds of underground tunnels.

DEEP CITY

The city had several floors, one on top of each other. The first (top) floor was used for animals, the second for churches and other floors were used for food storage and as living spaces.

FRESH AIR

A series of ventilation shafts run from the tunnels to the surface to give people access to fresh air. Wells for fresh water were dug into the floors of the tunnels.

HIDEOUT

Archaeologists think that about 3,500 people may have lived in Kaymakli at any one time, but that most people lived there temporarily in times of danger, rather than living underground all the time.

UNDERGROUND HIGHWAYS

A series of tunnels and chambers connects Kaymakli to another underground city called Derinkuyu, a few kilometres away.

Even today, some of the underground city is used as a storage space by local people.

SHAPING SETTLEMENTS

Human settlements are complicated - they require careful planning and management in order to be places where people can live healthy and happy lives. Good transport, reliable water and power supplies, affordable and safe housing, and healthy green spaces are some of the things an urban area needs to be a good place to live, as well as a good variety of jobs.

URBAN PLANNING

The process of planning and maintaining the healthy growth of settlements can be traced back to the ancient Egyptians and Mesopotamians. Today, urban planners and urban designers work with governments and residents to make cities and towns as healthy and successful as possible.

Urban planning includes making sure infrastructure, such as water pipes, is in place to support the settlement.

GO GREEN

Many of the people in charge of cities are working hard to make them as green, or environmentally friendly as possible. Encouraging people to use bicycles or public transport instead of cars cuts down air pollution. Building recycling facilities, saving water and using renewable energy are some of the ways of making cities cleaner.

Denmark's capital city, Copenhagen, has wind turbines along its coast supplying renewable energy to the city.

GET SMART

As urbanisation leads to bigger and bigger cities around the world, people are looking to technology for solutions to make them better places to live. So in a smart city, for instance, when a rubbish bin is full, a computer will send a message to the waste department to come and empty it.

These rubbish bins in Dubai contain sensors that let the waste department know when they are nearly full. The sensors are powered by built-in solar panels.

GET ACCESS

Urban planners around the world are beginning to provide more facilities for all the residents of their cities. This includes adding ramps and lifts to buses and metros for wheelchair users, adding beeps to pedestrian crossings for people who are partially sighted, and providing good access to public toilets.

OFF THE GRID

Some people choose to be as self-sufficient as possible, even if they live in larger settlements. People who live off-grid may generate their own electricity using solar or wind power, grow their own food and collect rainwater for drinking and washing.

A lot of people grow their own food in allotments, like this one in Urk in the Netherlands.

GLOSSARY

abandoned Deserted, left empty.

Aborigine The first people of Australia.

air pollution Air that has tiny bits of harmful or dirty materials or gases.

archaeologist Someone skilled in digging up sites where people have lived to discover their history.

archipelago A group of islands, often in a long line.

boom town A town that quickly grows in size.

border crossing The place on the border of two countries where people have their passports checked in order to move from one country to another.

capital The most important city in a country, usually the site of the national government.

Christian A member of the Christian Church.

climate The usual weather of an area.

conurbation Also called a metropolitan area, this describes where a city has expanded to absorb other smaller cities, towns and villages to become one urban area with a single name.

cormorant A large diving bird with a long neck.

council offices The buildings where the people who manage a town or city work.

crop A plant grown in large numbers for food.

employment Paid work.

environmentally friendly Not harmful to the environment (the natural world).

erosion When the action of waves, wind or water wears away the landscape or coastline.

facility A local facility could be a swimming pool or refuse collection, often provided by the local council.

geothermal energy Power produced by the internal heat of planet Earth.

hearth The place on the ground where people build a fire inside their home.

hydroelectric Using the power of moving water to generate electricity.

infrastructure Buildings, roads and public services (such as a power supply or drains).

inhabitant A person who lives in a place or country.

insulation A material that keeps something warm.

livestock An animal kept for food, such as a cow, pig or chicken.

loch A lake in Scotland.

medieval A period of history from the 5th to the 15th century.

Muslim A follower of the religion of Islam.

Neolithic Dating to the late Stone Age.

pack animal An animal used to transport goods, such as a horse, donkey or mule.

Parthian Empire A powerful empire in Persia (ancient Iraq and Iran) from 247 BCE to CE 224.

Phyrgia An ancient state in Turkey (1000 BCE-CE 1).

population All the people who live in a country or area.

port A harbour where ships load and unload goods.

predator An animal (or human) who hunts other animals to kill them.

prospector A person who searches for minerals, such as gold.

public transport Buses, trains, underground trains etc that run on set routes, with set ticket prices.

quarry A place where people dig stones and other materials out of the ground.

railway junction The place where several railway lines meet.

renewable energy Energy generated from renewable sources, such as wind, water or the Sun.

resources Land, sources of food, fire wood - what people need to survive.

Sasanian Empire A powerful empire in Persia (now Iraq and Iran) that lasted for over four hundred years from 224-651.

sauna A small room where people take a steam or hot-air bath to get clean.

savannah A wide area of open grassland.

services Shops, post offices, banks, schools, leisure centres, cinemas and hospitals.

sewage Waste water and human waste, carried in drains.

trade route The long-distance route used to transport goods to market.

well A shaft (or vertical passageway) down through the ground to reach ground water, such as a spring or underground river.

FURTHER INFORMATION

Books

Fact Planet: Settlements by Izzi Howell (Franklin Watts, 2020)

Geographics: Population and Settlement by Izzi Howell (Franklin Watts, 2017)

People and Planet Earth by Michael Bright (Wayland, 2016)

Websites

BBC bitesize about settlements:

www.bbc.co.uk/bitesize/topics/zx72pv4/articles/zrbvjhv

For more information about Skara Brae on Orkney, Scotland, go to:

www.natgeokids.com/uk/discover/history/general-history/skara-brae

The Royal Geographical Society has excellent school resources, such as Urban and Settlement:

www.rgs.org/schools/teaching-resources/urban-and-settlement

... and Rural Investigations:

www.rgs.org/schools/teaching-resources/rural-investigations

The website addresses (URLs) included in this book were valid at the time of going to press.

However, it is possible that contents or addresses may have changed since the publication of this book.

No responsibility for any such changes can be accepted by either the author or the Publisher.

INDEX

Franklin Watts
First published in Great Britain in 2020
by The Watts Publishing Group
Copyright © The Watts Publishing Group, 2020
All rights reserved

HB ISBN: 978 1 4451 6197 6
PB ISBN: 978 1 4451 6198 3

Editor: Paul Rockett
Illustrator: Paloma Valdivia
Designer: Lisa Peacock
Picture Researcher: Diana Morris

Franklin Watts
An imprint of Hachette Children's Group
Part of The Watts Publishing Group
Carmelite House
50 Victoria Embankment
London EC4Y 0DZ
An Hachette UK Company

The publisher would like to thank the following for permission to
reproduce their pictures:

Alamy: Aerial Archives 12t; Dan Leeth 18t; Kilian O'Sullivan 10t;
Vivienne Sharp/Imagestate/Impact 14t; Dreamstime: Nancy
Dressel 7b; Chris Lofty 4t; iStock: Ronald Nelson Photography
16t; Pakhnyushchyy 26t; Shutterstock: Aoshi VN 4b; aphotostory
6t; Asia Travel 5c; Harry Beuhelink 5t; Scott Biales 20t; Ronnie
Chua 24t; dibrova 5b; duchy 8t; F11 Photo 22t; GLF Media
7t; Industry & Travel 28b; Ioan Panaite 29t; riopatuca 29c; Serato
28c; Sundry Photography 7c; testing 6b; T W van Urk 29b.

Every attempt has been made to clear copyright. Should there
be any inadvertent omission please apply to the publisher for
rectification.

www.hachette.co.uk
www.franklinwatts.co.uk

Printed in Dubai